ORCA
FOOTPRINTS

Design Like Nature

BIOMIMICRY FOR A HEALTHY PLANET

MEGAN CLENDENAN
KIM RYALL WOOLCOCK

ORCA BOOK PUBLISHERS

Published in Canada and the United States
in 2021 by Orca Book Publishers.
orcabook.com

Library and Archives Canada Cataloguing in Publication
Title: Design like nature : biomimicry for a healthy planet / Megan Clendenan, Kim Ryall Woolcock.
Names: Clendenan, Megan, 1977- author. | Woolcock, Kim Ryall, author.
Series: Orca footprints.
Description: Series statement: Orca footprints | Includes bibliographical references and index.
Identifiers: Canadiana (print) 20200271709 | Canadiana (ebook) 20200271717 | isbn 9781459824645 (hardcover) | isbn 9781459824652 (pdf) | isbn 9781459824669 (epub)
Subjects: lcsh: Biomimicry—Juvenile literature. | lcsh: Technological innovations—Juvenile literature.
Classification: lcc t173.8 .c44 2021 | ddc j600—dc23

Library of Congress Control Number: 2020939213

Summary: Part of the nonfiction Orca Footprints series for middle readers, in this book young readers discover innovations and inventions inspired by nature.

Orca Book Publishers is committed to reducing the consumption of nonrenewable resources in the making of our books. We make every effort to use materials that support a sustainable future.

Orca Book Publishers gratefully acknowledges the support for its publishing programs provided by the following agencies: the Government of Canada, the Canada Council for the Arts and the Province of British Columbia through the BC Arts Council and the Book Publishing Tax Credit.

Front cover images by gkuna/Getty Images and Mischa Keijser/Getty Images
Back cover images by KPWangkanont/Shutterstock.com, Mr.B-king/Shutterstock.com and Louis Hansel/Unsplash.com
Design by Teresa Bubela
Layout by Dahlia Yuen
Edited by Kirstie Hudson

Printed and bound in China.

24 23 22 21 • 1 2 3 4

Fireflies naturally glow at night! Nature designs in a way that doesn't waste or pollute—and even seems a bit magical.
TOMMY TSUTSUI/GETTY IMAGES

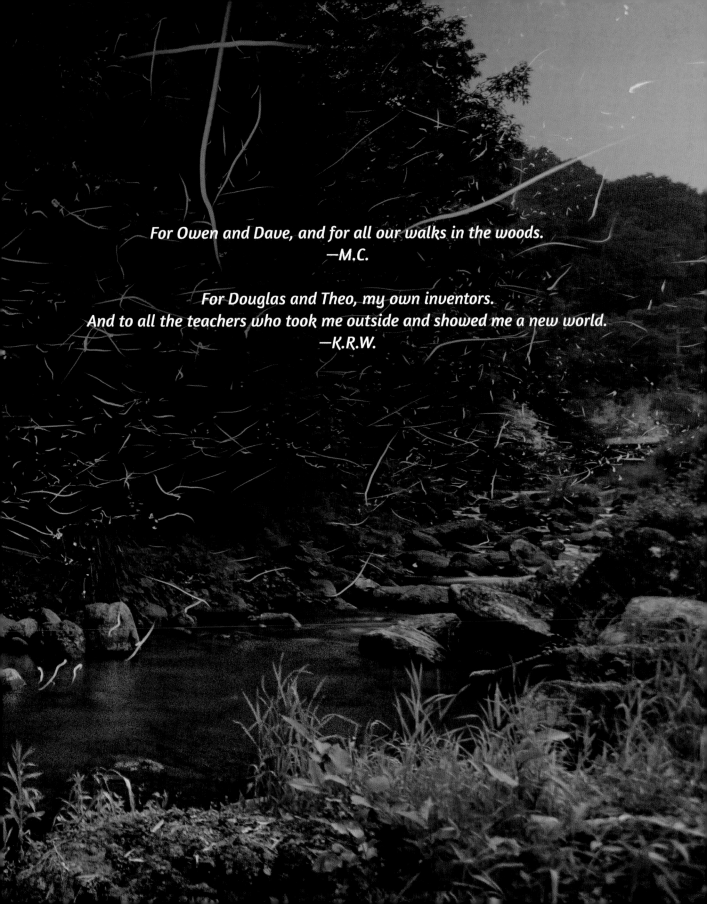

For Owen and Dave, and for all our walks in the woods.
—M.C.

For Douglas and Theo, my own inventors.
And to all the teachers who took me outside and showed me a new world.
—K.R.W.

Contents

Introduction **6**

CHAPTER ONE
INVENTIONS GONE WILD

How Does Nature Design? 8
Natural Materials 10
Royal Purple 10
From Parachutes to Toothbrushes 12
Oily Outfit 12
Miracle Material...or Not? 13
Flying Fruit 14
There is No "Away" 15
A Lawn Where the Cactus Should Be 15

CHAPTER TWO
NATURE AS ENGINEER

It's Easy Being Green 16
Pull Yourself Together! 18
Stuck on You 19
Green Chemistry 19
Powerful Patterns 20
Brainless Chatter 22
Clean as Dirt 22
Nature's Apprentices 23

CHAPTER THREE
ASKING ADVICE FROM NATURE

Psst...Hey Nature...What Would You Do? 24

From Beaks to Bullet Trains 25

Nicer Needles 26

Sugar-Coated Medicines 26

Spotless as Shark Skin 27

Light It Up, Firefly 27

Super-Sticky Gecko Tape 28

Catch the Rain(water) 28

Stronger Than Steel, Made Like Yogurt 29

Roaches to the Rescue! 29

Cat-Brained Computing 30

Batteries from Beaches? 31

CHAPTER FOUR
REDUCING OUR FOOTPRINT

Looking Back to Look Forward 32

Nature's Building Blocks 34

Forest in the City 35

Chill Out... 36

Germs Dyed My Clothes 37

Fishy Wind Farms 38

Watch, Learn, Invent 38

The Land of Tomorrow 41

Acknowledgments 42

Resources 43

Glossary 44

Index 46

Introduction

Seashells are not just strong—they come in just about every size, shape and color you can imagine. How's that for great design?
VIKTORIIANOVOKHATSKA/GETTY IMAGES

Have you ever held a seashell and wondered how its delicate swirl can be so strong? Or lay down under a tree so tall it touches the clouds and wondered how it withstands the strongest winds? Nature is a genius at design.

Humans love to design too. We build huge cities, create all kinds of chemicals and make tons of electronics and plastics. But the way we design is changing our climate and creating unmanageable amounts of garbage.

What if we could learn to design like nature instead? What would it be like if we could build houses like sea creatures build their shells? Dye our clothes with *germs* instead of chemicals? Or make lights that run on glowing *bacteria* instead of electricity?

Inventors, designers and kids are all asking advice from nature and working on innovations that will let us live in better harmony with our world. Want to see how? Grab your friends and your magnifying glass and come take a peek inside nature's toolbox!

Once my husband and I went on a six-month-long camping trip. Our only shelter was our tent. We woke with the sun and went to bed as it got dark. We didn't waste a drop of water. We fit ourselves into the natural cycle. But we sometimes wished for a warm room and a large pizza! DAVE CLENDENAN

Sometimes I shower with a tree frog. My family is building a house on a forested hill, and for now our shower is outside. Tiny green tree frogs like to hang out in it on hot days, leaning against my damp facecloth to stay cool. Sharing my shower with these delicate creatures has made me think hard about how we treat our planet. DOUGLAS WOOLCOCK

TEEKAYGEE/SHUTTERSTOCK.COM

CHAPTER ONE

Inventions Gone Wild

The secrets to a sustainable world are all around us.

—Janine Benyus, cofounder, The Biomimicry Institute

HOW DOES NATURE DESIGN?

Biomimicry is the scientific term for copying nature, not only to solve human problems but also to help protect our planet. *Bio* means "life" and *mimicry* means "the action of imitating," so put them together and you've got the science of copying nature. Everything from the largest mammals to the tiniest bacteria has spent millions of years figuring out how to work with the natural cycles of the planet.

It's pretty neat that nature runs on sunlight and water. Humans, on the other hand, use *fossil fuels* and *toxic* chemicals. Nature wastes nothing, but humans have left garbage pretty much everywhere on Earth. The great news is, we can change our ways. There are solutions. We just have to ask nature.

Take something as common as a leaf. A leaf gains its energy to grow from the sun. By studying the structure of a leaf, we can learn more about how the leaf does this. Then we can take our

There's more to a leaf than we can see at first glance. KYRYL GORLOV/GETTY IMAGES

Children of all ages have come up with inventions and designs that help protect the environment.
ARIEL SKELLEY/GETTY IMAGES

new knowledge one step further and apply it to something we need, such as a more efficient ***solar panel***. There are scientists working on that idea right now.

If we want to know how to make less-toxic glue or how to create brilliant color, nature is a fantastic teacher. When engineers, designers, architects or scientists look to nature to solve problems, they are using biomimicry.

Humans love to invent, and we've dreamed up many amazing things to make our lives easier and better. It's hard to imagine a world without computers and cars. But at the same time, our creations have changed our climate and polluted our world. Before we dive in to learning how nature designs, let's look at how humans have gone from fitting into the environment by using what's available to taking too many resources from the earth without thinking about what might happen in the future, and how the explosion of new technologies and materials has changed our world—for good and for bad.

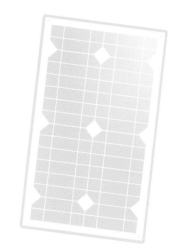

The Coast Salish Peoples of southern British Columbia traditionally used a type of reed called a scouring rush, also known as horsetail, as a natural toothbrush.
TIKTA ALIK/SHUTTERSTOCK.COM

During testing some of the arrows bounced off the armor—but this one didn't!
GREG ALDRETE

NATURAL MATERIALS

Can you imagine playing soccer with a ball made of tree sap? Or growing the material for your T-shirt and then dyeing it with smashed bugs? For as long as we have been around, about 300,000 years, humans have been making tools, clothing and houses. Until just a few hundred years ago, all the materials had to be gathered from the natural world—stone, bone, wood, plants, animals and insects. Clothes could only be made from natural materials such as woven cotton, wool or **linen**, or leather from animal skins, in mostly gray, brown or off-white colors. Buttons were made of materials such as shell or metal and were so costly that only the wealthy could afford them. There were no plastic toothbrushes. Instead people used toothbrushes made of sticks with brush-like ends or wild-boar hairs carefully threaded through handles drilled with small holes.

When we think of armor, we usually think of metal suits or chain mail. But the ancient Greeks had cloth armor! First they made linen from the fibers of the flax plant. Then they stuck 30 layers of the fabric together with a glue made from rabbit skins. The armor was light and comfortable but could stop any arrow. When modern-day researchers made a copy of this ancient armor, they trusted it enough to wear it while getting shot with an arrow!

ROYAL PURPLE

But natural materials have some limitations. They wear out. They get moldy. They can be heavy or smelly or hard to make. And sometimes it is difficult to harvest enough material to make enough armor or toothbrushes or clothing dye for a whole village, never mind a huge city.

Take dye, for example. We consider it perfectly normal to go to the store and pick out a shirt in any color imaginable. But for most of human history, clothes were dyed with roots, berries, bark or leaves, or not dyed at all, so they weren't as colorful as they are now. Certain colors, like purple, were so hard to make that only royalty could afford purple clothing. These days a purple shirt isn't harder to find or more expensive than one in another color.

But in Roman times only emperors wore purple. The dye was made from snails. Thousands of snails were collected, and then each shell was cracked and the slime inside was squeezed out. The slime was left in the sun until it turned purple—it had to be left for just the right amount of time. If it was left for too long, it would turn dark red. While the slime was changing color, it smelled terrible.

Things changed in 1856 when William Henry Perkin, who was trying to make a medicine to fight **malaria**, accidentally made black gunk that turned fabric brilliant purple. No snails needed! He built a factory and made enough dye so that purple clothes weren't just for royalty anymore.

The dye made from these ocean-dwelling snails (Hexaplex trunculus) was worth more than its weight in gold.
FABRIC: MARINA KRYNOCHKINA/SHUTTERSTOCK.COM
SHELL: JAMES ST. JOHN/FLICKR.COM/CC BY 2.0

FACT:
To make natural dyes stick to fabrics, people used to soak clothes in *stale urine*!

A woman in Chinchero, Peru, is using smashed cochineal insects, leaves and flowers to dye handmade wool fabric.
MABELIN SANTOS/SHUTTERSTOCK.COM

Nylon helps adventurers around the world fly high. VVOEVALE/DREAMSTIME.COM

Before synthetics were invented, people protected themselves from rain with materials like wool, rubber and even straw. Raincoats today are lightweight, quick-drying and fun to wear in puddles! DAVE CLENDENAN

FROM PARACHUTES TO TOOTHBRUSHES

Nylon is a plastic that can be molded into almost anything imaginable, including clothes and toothbrushes. When it was launched at the 1939 New York World's Fair, it changed the world. In the 1940s, many countries were fighting in World War II. They needed materials to help them fight the war, and plastic turned up at just the right time. It could be used for lightweight airplane parts, helmets, fuel tanks and flak jackets (protective vests). Now nylon is everywhere. Kevlar is a super-strong synthetic material similar to nylon used to make such things as bulletproof vests, tires and bike locks.

In 1942 Adeline Gray became the first person to use a nylon parachute. Before World War II, parachutes had been made of *silk*. But because silk came from Japan, one of the Allies' opponents in the war, it was no longer available. So nylon stepped in. It was considered "the fiber that won the war" for the Allies.

OILY OUTFIT

Would you be surprised to hear that many of your clothes, shoes and jackets are made from oil? When you pull on a waterproof rain jacket, stretchy sports pants or running shoes, you've got polyester to thank. Like nylon, polyester is a *synthetic fiber* made from coal, water and petroleum, and it's manufactured in a laboratory. Other kinds of plastic get turned into clothing too. Fleece fabric is made from recycled clear plastic water bottles. The bottles are melted, spun into thread and woven into cozy fabric.

MIRACLE MATERIAL...OR NOT?

We know that plastic is a super-handy material—strong, water-proof, lightweight and able to be stretched into almost any shape we like. And because it's easy and fairly cheap, we can produce as much of it as we want. When we used natural materials, we were limited by how much we could hunt or harvest. Today we produce around 350 million tons (317 metric tons) of plastic each year.

Plastic in all its forms, including synthetic fibers, is convenient and easy to use. But it has created some big new problems. We throw most of it in the trash after using it a single time, and once there it doesn't decompose for a long time.

Consider plastic drinking straws—you need one for about 10 minutes, but it will last 500 years or longer. Plastic shopping bags, which became popular in the 1980s, are now produced at a rate of one trillion bags a year, and they too last hundreds of years. Synthetic fibers also won't decompose for 20 to 200 years, so the polyester sweater you don't like anymore will end up in the landfill next to that plastic shopping bag you used once.

Tiny bits of plastic are now found everywhere on Earth. Microplastics, which are pieces of plastic smaller than 3/16 of an inch (five millimeters), break off synthetic clothes in the washing machine and enter our food and water. DAVID PEREIRAS/SHUTTERSTOCK.COM

COPY THAT, COPYCAT

If you look around your home, you will probably find plastics everywhere. In the shiny television and computer. In your toaster, kettle and fridge. The washing machine. The hair dryer in your bathroom. Almost all electrical appliances are made with some kind of plastic because it does not **conduct** electricity and can withstand high heat, so it helps prevent electric shock and fire. Look around your house and see what's natural and what's synthetic.

Kim's friends grow so much food in their garden that they keep some in their root cellar to eat in winter. DAN KALF

FLYING FRUIT

Before fridges, people stored their food in all sorts of creative ways—in cellars, outdoor window boxes, even underwater in nearby streams or wells. They spent time salting, smoking and pickling food to eat over the winter. Sometimes people even hung up their vegetables, like Christmas stockings, by the fire to dry. Once fridges and refrigerated trucks were invented, grocery stores brimmed with out-of-season foods all year, flown or trucked in from countries around the world.

Consider your after-school snack. Maybe you have strawberries that come in a plastic package, or you peel a banana from Ecuador. While it's nice to have fresh fruit in December, these foods have been transported thousands of miles. More than 3 million tons (2.7 million metric tons) of bananas are shipped to the United States each year. Bananas coming from Ecuador have to travel more than 4,000 miles (6,400 kilometers) to reach our grocery stores in the Pacific Northwest.

Our fridges and refrigerated trucks do more than keep our milk and vegetables cold. They also contain toxic chemicals and

NATURE'S JOURNAL

For Pioneer Day at school, Kim's son had to bring a lunch a pioneer could have packed. No store-bought granola bars, no thermos full of hot mac and cheese, no ziplock baggie of raisins—not even bananas or oranges, because they come from so far away. He took a baked potato still in its skin, and a piece of bread and a chunk of cheese wrapped in fabric coated with beeswax. Students made butter at school by shaking whipping cream in mason jars. Kim's son said it was one of his most delicious lunches ever! If we all went back to eating like this, think how good it would be for the planet!

Theo's favorite part was the bread with fresh butter. KIM RYALL WOOLCOCK

Cell phones are made of rare metals that are difficult and dangerous to extract. After all that effort, most cell phones aren't recycled.
BEEBOYS/SHUTTERSTOCK.COM

emit greenhouse gases that heat up our planet. And when fridges get old, we need to get rid of them. But how?

THERE IS NO 'AWAY'

When we throw things away, they don't just vanish. When we get rid of our old fridge, it ends up in the landfill, next to the polyester sweater and the plastic bag. Waste is piling up in those places. And there's another problem too. Take cell phones and computers. They feel clean in our hands, but they are made of toxic and hard-to-get materials. Electronic waste leaks toxic chemicals into the soil and water, harming both people and the environment. Around the world, we produce 55 million tons (50 million metric tons) of e-waste each year. That's equal to the weight of 5,500 Eiffel Towers!

A LAWN WHERE THE CACTUS SHOULD BE

Birds are amazing creatures. Some birds nest in hollows in cliffs. Others build their nests out of mud or sticks. They take what they need from nearby trees and plants. But people often try to change their environment instead of working with what's there.

It takes a ton of energy to change a place to suit ourselves instead of living in harmony with our surroundings. The desert city of Las Vegas, Nevada, gets about 4.5 inches (115 millimeters) of rain each year, so much of its water is pumped in from Lake Mead, located more than 30 miles (48 kilometers) away. Some of that distance is uphill. If you've ever tried to lift a big bucket of water, you know that water is heavy. Huge pumps lift and carry more than one million gallons of water per minute to Las Vegas. The pumps use $38 million in electricity per year. Some of this water is used to keep lawns green. But maybe we could think differently. Perhaps we don't need a lawn if we live in the desert. We could have a cactus garden instead.

Imagine if you could live in a house that looked like this!
PLATOO FOTOGRAPHY/SHUTTERSTOCK.COM

CHAPTER TWO

Nature as Engineer

Slender, tapering cone, heavily resinous

Solar energy not exceeding 1000 watts per square meter

Branches flexible & whorled

Soft, flexible, blue-green needles

Grey-brown, deeply furrowed bark

Trunk circumference 8'

Chemical Compund Structure

Well-drained, slightly acidic soil

No discernible taproot

30'

FACT:

The scales on butterfly wings are shaped to reflect light, creating brilliant color without dyes or *pigments*.

Each scale on the wings of this painted lady butterfly (Vanessa cardui) is a single color.
DR. NIPAM PATEL

IT'S EASY BEING GREEN

The world around us is always changing. Every spring, trees make a whole new set of leaves, and every fall those same leaves become waste. The tree doesn't have to take those leaves to the recycling depot or throw them in the trash. It just drops them on the ground right below it, where all the insects and *fungi* and bacteria feast on them, turning them into fresh, nutrient-rich soil. The tree will soak up those same nutrients and use them to make its next batch of leaves. Just like humans, nature is always using energy, building things and making waste. But nature has been doing it for billions of years, and doing it in a way that doesn't create more problems. Maybe we need to take a look at nature's solutions and use biomimicry to solve some of our own problems.

Nature runs on sunlight

If you lie in the sun, it warms you. This might not seem significant. But that warming energy is powerful—it feeds the whole planet. When the sun's rays hit plant leaves, the plants capture

Gardening is a great opportunity to watch plants grow and see photosynthesis in action.
TINNAPONG/SHUTTERSTOCK.COM

the energy and use it to spin sugar out of thin air by combining **carbon dioxide** with water in a process called **photosynthesis**. The plants use this sugar as their food. The plants are food for all plant-eating animals. And the plant-eating animals are the food for the meat eaters. Unlike humans, who are using fossil fuels, polluting the planet and causing **climate change**, nature runs on an energy source that doesn't run out and doesn't pollute.

Nature makes amazing materials

When we think of inventors or engineers, we usually think of humans, not insects. But many creatures make structures and materials that are better designed than anything we can create. For example, think of a potato-chip bag. It has a fancy design on the outside, it's strong enough to protect the chips during transport, and it keeps bacteria and water out.

Most chip bags need about seven layers of different materials to do that, all made in factories using chemicals. Insects do something similar, but they do it better than we do. They build their **exoskeletons** out of just one material called **chitin**, and it is waterproof, breathable, strong, durable and beautiful.

Hair combs used to be made out of "tortoiseshell," a beautiful, durable material similar to plastic. But people wouldn't feel comfortable today knowing that hawksbill sea turtles had to be killed just to make a comb.
COMB: COURTESY OF COOPER HEWITT, SMITHSONIAN DESIGN MUSEUM
SEA TURTLE: DAVDEKA/SHUTTERSTOCK.COM

Vegetable and garden scraps can be turned back into soil by composting them.
MEGWALLACEPHOTOGRAPHY/DREAMSTIME.COM

The beautiful blue-green layer inside this shell, called mother-of-pearl, is what makes it so strong. JOSHUADANIEL/SHUTTERSTOCK.COM

Ants self-organize into bridges without a leader or a plan and dissolve the bridges as soon as traffic slows.
FRANK60/SHUTTERSTOCK.COM

FACT:
Ants cluster to form buoyant rafts and aerial bridges, building structures with their bodies.

Nature reuses everything

Nature is the ultimate recycler. The oxygen you're breathing is the same **molecules** that have been making their rounds of Earth for billions of years. Some of the air in your lungs right now might have been breathed by a dinosaur millions of years ago. The **carbon** in our food, the **nitrogen** in plants—all these molecules are cycled endlessly around the planet.

PULL YOURSELF TOGETHER!

Your cocoa mug is surprisingly similar to the space shuttle. They're both made of super-tough ceramic. Ceramics are hard and can handle high temperatures, so they're good for making mugs that last for years and tiles that could protect the space shuttle against intense heat.

But it takes tons of energy to make ceramics. They have to be baked at 2300°F (1260°C), and although they are very hard, they are also brittle and shatter easily—think of dropping a dinner plate.

Some creatures make shells that are super hard and almost impossible to shatter, and they do it without factories or furnaces. What's their secret? They let the pieces put themselves together.

Abalone are sea snails with soft bodies and super-tough shells. To build their shells, abalone excrete a layer of squishy **protein** speckled with tiny crystals. The crystals act like magnets, pulling in **minerals** from the seawater to harden the shell. Thanks to electrical and chemical attraction, the minerals click together, making the shell super strong. Your bones and teeth are built this way too.

Researchers are working on designing **self-assembling materials**. Imagine if you could spray the roof of your house with a liquid that self-assembled into solar cells to capture the sun's rays, providing all the power you needed!

STUCK ON YOU

You probably use Velcro fasteners every day, on your shoes, coat or backpack. They're easy to open and close and can be reused almost infinitely. Velcro is everywhere, and it was inspired by nature. In 1941 inventor George de Mestral was walking in the Swiss Alps. When he got home, he noticed how many burrs (plant seeds) were stuck to his clothes and his dog. He might simply have thought this was a problem. Instead, curious, he looked at them under the microscope. He saw that the hooks of the burrs were stuck in the loops of his woven clothes and tangled in the hairs of his dog's fur. He decided to make a fastener in the same way, using hooks and loops. He called it Velcro.

GREEN CHEMISTRY

When Megan was 11, she received a chemistry kit for her birthday and got to make frothy, red lava and purple slime. This was a great gift! Chemistry sets often come with gloves and goggles because some of the chemicals can burn your skin or irritate your eyes. That's one way to do chemistry. But if you've ever seen a firefly light up the night with its glow, you've seen that chemistry can also be nontoxic. Fireflies combine a nontoxic chemical with oxygen, using an **enzyme**, to produce their glow— without heat or toxic byproducts. When humans mimic how nature does chemistry, we call it green chemistry.

This dog might be hoping that unhooking the burrs goes as easily as hooking them!

NATURE'S JOURNAL

Glue is great, but it doesn't work when it's wet. When you go to a dock, you'll see that marine life like mussels, anemones and feather duster worms glue themselves to underwater things and hang on, even in pounding waves. Kim and her family know just how well these critters stick. They have to clean the bottom of their small boat all the time, even though it is coated with special slippery paint meant to prevent anything from growing on it. But these creatures are so good at sticking themselves to surfaces that after even a few days in summer, the bottom of the boat is covered with **algae**, and if they leave it there too long, barnacles and mussels appear.

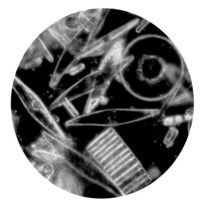

Spicy mustard can surprise us by making our eyes water and our noses sting.
PETROVICH NATALIYA/SHUTTERSTOCK.COM

Like plants, diatoms gain energy from the sun. These tiny marine creatures produce about 20 to 50 percent of the world's oxygen.
PROF. GORDON T. TAYLOR/NSF POLAR PROGRAMS/NOAA

FACT:
A fractal is a geometric pattern that repeats and looks the same at any scale. Fractals help scientists identify patterns such as brain waves, bacterial growth and wireless cell signals!

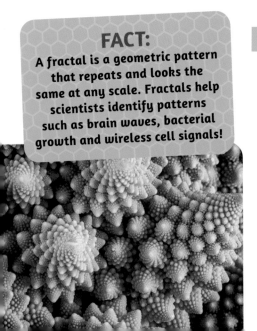

Mustard bomb

Have you felt the sting of spicy mustard? The sting is not there just for good taste. In fact, it's meant as a defense. Mustard plants taste the way they do to defend themselves against insects that want to eat them. The plants produce anti-insect chemicals that are too nasty to store in their own *cells*—they would hurt themselves if they did! The solution? Separate the chemical into harmless molecules and store them in two separate cells. When a bug bites, tearing open those cells, the molecules come together to produce an anti-insect chemical so powerful that researchers call it "the mustard oil bomb"!

Ice, ice, baby

Tiny ocean creatures called ice diatoms live in freezing-cold seawater. Ice can form sharp crystals, and to a tiny creature like a diatom, these crystals are deadly spears. To stop the ice crystals around it from growing right through its body, the diatom secretes a protein that interlocks with the ice crystal points like a 3-D puzzle, stopping them from growing. By keeping the crystals around it small, the diatom doesn't get speared. This chemical trick allows the diatoms to survive in an icy environment that would kill most creatures.

POWERFUL PATTERNS

When you observe the stitches in your socks or the waves in the sea, you're seeing a pattern. A pattern is a design that repeats in a structured way. Patterns in nature aren't just for looks. They help things work better with less energy. For many plants and animals, patterns can be the difference between surviving or not.

Romanesco broccoli is a great example of a fractal, plus it's tasty and full of vitamins. SIMON BRATT/SHUTTERSTOCK.COM

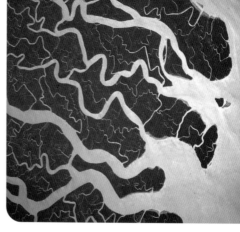

Branching out

If you were to lie under a tree and look up, you might notice that the trunk splits into branches, and then each branch splits again into more branches. This is known as a branching pattern. What do river deltas and the human lung have in common with tree branches? They are all built on a branching pattern. Branching patterns are everywhere because they are so effective at gathering and distributing rain, water or air. This means that all the parts of the structure—whether it's a tree, lung or river delta—can get the water or nutrients they need to survive.

This image of the Ganges River delta in Bangladesh and India was taken by the space shuttle Columbia. *The branching pattern goes for hundreds of miles!* COURTESY OF NASA

Round and round we go

You don't have to look far to see spiral patterns. You find them in everything from snail shells to hurricanes. A spiral starts on a center point and then curves around and around. Spirals are designed for protection. Fern fronds—the long, divided leaves of ferns—are wound tightly to protect them from being chomped on while they're growing. Spirals act as funnels, guiding things where they should go. Your ear is shaped like a shell, funneling sound to the eardrum inside, which detects sound waves. And spirals also store energy like springs do.

Spiral muscles let a chameleon shoot out its tongue five times faster than a fighter jet accelerates. CATHY KEIFER/SHUTTERSTOCK.COM

Fibonacci

Can flowers do math? They sure can't do your division homework, but mathematical patterns that reflect the Fibonacci sequence are everywhere in nature. In the Fibonacci sequence each number is the sum of the previous two. Thus you have 0, 1, 1, 2, 3, 5, 8, 13, 21, 34, 55, 89, 144 and so on to infinity. To pack in the most seeds possible, sunflower seeds are arranged in spiral patterns that reflect the Fibonacci sequence. This pattern allows the closest possible packing of seeds. These same spirals are found in pineapples, pine cones and nautilus shells, to name a few.

Patterns are everywhere in nature—fractals, spirals, spots and stripes, **vortexes**. Go see what you can find!

Do you think this nautilus needed to use a calculator to figure out how to grow?
DANNY IACOB/SHUTTERSTOCK.COM

Challenge your friends to build something with you without using any words!
MONKEYBUSINESSIMAGES/GETTY IMAGES

BRAINLESS CHATTER

If you and a friend were building a fort outside, you'd probably talk about the materials you needed to gather, how many big branches, how many small, how you would connect everything. But if you didn't have a voice, or even a brain, it sure would be difficult to communicate your plan for the fort.

You might be surprised by how much hidden communication happens in the forest. Slimy yellow blobs slither and slink in all directions, eating leaves and mulch. Are they plants? Animals? Fungi? Turns out, none of the above. They're slime molds.

The slime mold is an amoeba, a brainless, single-celled organism. No feet? No problem. Slime molds can travel a long way. One researcher discovered a slime mold in New Zealand that was identical to ones found in the United States.

Scientists have also discovered that a slime mold can learn, even though it doesn't have a brain. In laboratory tests, slime molds learned to avoid substances they didn't like, including caffeine, and find what they did like. Turns out their favorite food is oats!

Researchers at the University of Hokkaido in Japan placed pieces of oatmeal to represent railway stations, then released the slime molds. The molds spread out and formed a network a lot like the real-world Tokyo rail system! This experiment shows great promise as a biomimicry tool for mapping efficient road systems, as the slime mold always finds the most efficient route between two places.

CLEAN AS DIRT

There's a type of bacteria (Mycobacterium vaccae) found in dirt that can boost your mood—no wonder it feels so good to play in the mud. FATCAMERA/GETTY IMAGES

We usually think of water as clean, and dirt as, well, *dirty*. You use water to wash dirt off your hands and your clothes. But did you know that dirt is what cleans your water?

Soil is the biggest natural filter on the planet. It acts like a huge sieve or sponge. As water from rain or streams passes through the millions of tiny tubes and pores in the soil, the dirt holds on to pollutants such as harmful chemicals and minerals, letting only clean water through.

Trees do the same thing for the air. Trees remove **particulate matter**, a major health hazard, from the atmosphere. Some plants slurp up **heavy metals** from soils. Valuable metals can sometimes be extracted after the plants are harvested, which is called **phytomining**.

We can use germs to help with this, too. Scientists have found that many types of bacteria can remove heavy metals and other pollutants from water and soil. For example, bacteria were used to clean up London's Olympic Park. The area was heavily polluted after being used for industry for hundreds of years. So **microbes** were added to the soil and groundwater. After the bacteria did their cleanup, the site was used to host the 2012 Olympic and Paralympic Games.

NATURE'S APPRENTICES

So nature has a few tricks up its sleeve to keep everything running smoothly. Using what we've learned from diatoms, mustard and brainless molds, scientists are already exploring how biomimicry can help us restore the planet instead of damaging it.

COPY THAT, COPYCAT

Heroes of nature! Sketch, photograph or journal about an amazing creature that can do something you can't. Do some research on the creature to discover its superpowers. Notice ant highways, leaves that spin sugar out of sunlight and fungi that can eat trees.

NATURE'S JOURNAL

Many years ago Megan and her husband went canoeing in the Okefenokee Swamp, located in the southern United States. The water was black...and filled with alligators! The park ranger told them not to worry because in late winter alligators like to lie still and soak up the sunshine. That day they saw more alligators than they could count. The animals were splayed on logs, nestled among lily pads and camouflaged in thick shrubs. Megan and her husband didn't know that they were paddling through one of nature's greatest cleaning tools. A swamp is just another name for a wetland, and wetlands are one of nature's best water-filtration systems. Wetlands contain natural bacteria that offer nutrition to plants and remove nitrogen, helping the ecosystem function at its best.

Here's Megan paddling through a giant cleaning station—a swamp! Do you keep an alligator in your cleaning cupboard?
DAVE CLENDENAN

CHAPTER THREE

Asking Advice from Nature

PSST...HEY NATURE... WHAT WOULD YOU DO?

You never know what you might discover when you look close up at nature.
ALL_ABOUT_PEOPLE/SHUTTERSTOCK.COM

FACT:
Hippopotamuses ooze a natural oil that prevents them from getting sunburned. One day our sunscreens might be inspired by hippo sweat!

Imagine you've just spilled a big blob of ketchup on your favorite shirt. You wanted to wear it to a birthday party tomorrow. You might be wondering if the stain will ever come out. But what if the fabric designer had first asked how nature stays clean?

Lotus plants stay squeaky clean even though they live in muddy swamps. The surfaces of the plants are rough and allow water to flow off without sticking. The water removes dirt, dust and mud as it goes.

By learning more about how this works, scientists can develop products that mimic the lotus plants, resulting in easier cleanup and fewer chemicals. One great idea already underway is clothing fabric that repels stains from coffee, mustard and, yes, ketchup!

Sometimes by looking at a problem in a new way, we can find a better solution. If we observe nature's genius, we might discover new answers to old problems, just waiting to be noticed.

The new train goes 10 percent faster on 15 percent less electricity.
MAHATHIR MOHD YASIN/SHUTTERSTOCK.COM

FROM BEAKS TO BULLET TRAINS

Trains in Japan travel fast, up to 185 miles (300 kilometers) per hour. They used to be shaped like bullets to make them **aerodynamic**. But there was a problem. When the trains went through tunnels, a wave of air pressure built up in front of them, making a booming sound that woke neighbors and disturbed wildlife. Engineers were tasked with designing a quieter, more aerodynamic train.

One of the engineers working on the problem was also a birder. At a birders' meeting one day he saw a film of a kingfisher diving into the water beak first without creating a splash. Kingfishers have big heads and long, narrow beaks that enable them to dive into the water without creating any ripples. This allows them to see their prey as they dive to catch it for dinner. The engineer realized that the train needed to copy the kingfisher and dive into the tunnels without creating a splash of sound. He shaped the front of the train like the kingfisher beak—and it worked!

Kingfishers can reach speeds of up to 25 miles per hour (40 kilometers per hour) when diving. PETR SIMON/SHUTTERSTOCK.COM

Imagine if needle shots hurt as little as mosquito bites.

CHAKKRACHAI NICHARAT/SHUTTERSTOCK.COM

FACT:
Woodpeckers whack their beaks into trees hard enough to break wood. Humans get a concussion if they are hit just one-tenth as hard. By studying how woodpeckers protect their brains, engineers designed shock absorbers that can be used for such things as helping spacecraft resist impacts from small objects in space.

To reach people everywhere, vaccines must be transported on roads that can be hard to find! When Kim and her husband drove through South America, they once had to get on top of the van with binoculars to find the way.

KIM RYALL WOOLCOCK

NICER NEEDLES

Mosquitos don't want to be noticed when they bite—if they are, they might get squashed! Over millions of years, mosquito mouths have evolved to steal blood as stealthily as possible. Researchers have taken a close look at those mouths to figure out how biomimicry could make nicer needles for injecting medicine.

The resulting needles are tiny, only one-tenth the size of the usual ones. They are less painful because they vibrate, like a knife sliding back and forth to cut bread, and the nurse doesn't have to push as hard to make them break the skin. Because these needles make shots less painful, they may be especially helpful to people who need many injections every day, such as people with diabetes.

SUGAR-COATED MEDICINES

Vaccines can prevent all sorts of diseases, from measles and mumps to cholera. But if vaccines get too hot, they don't work anymore. Refrigerating them as they are transported on planes, trains and automobiles from the lab where they were made to destinations all over the globe is tricky and requires a lot of energy! Many vaccines are destroyed during transport.

In tackling this issue, scientists were inspired by tiny creatures called tardigrades, also known as water bears. Tardigrades are one-fifth the size of a flea, and they have been found everywhere on Earth, even in the harshest environments, from the bottom of the deepest oceans to the tops of Earth's coldest peaks. They survive by drying out completely, going without food or water for up to 120 years. As soon as they get wet again, they come right back to life, no damage done!

The secret is in their sugars, specifically one called trehalose. When most cells dry out, they collapse. Water bears protect theirs by coating them with a super-thin layer of trehalose. The sugar forms a smooth, glassy coating that safeguards everything inside. When scientists tried the same technique with vaccines, it worked! Sugar-coated vaccines can last for up to six months with no refrigeration.

Astronauts exposed dehydrated tardigrades to the vacuum of space—and they survived.
3DSTOCK/SHUTTERSTOCK.COM

SPOTLESS AS SHARK SKIN

If you saw a whale up close, you'd probably find it covered with a layer of crusty barnacles. Sometimes the barnacles are so thick they're like a suit of armor. But sharks are usually sleek and smooth. Tiny scales called denticles make shark skin feel like very fine sandpaper and keep barnacles at bay.

Scientists have created a germ-repelling surface that mimics shark skin. The surface is covered with millions of microscopic, diamond-shaped scales, packed so close together that it's hard for disease-causing bacteria to settle between the lumps and bumps.

A sheet of "shark skin" can be placed over surfaces in germ-prone areas like hospitals, public bathrooms, science labs and even childcare centers. Because the disease-causing bacteria can't stick to the rough surface, they can't grow. Fewer harmful bacteria without the use of **antibiotics**— shark skin for the win!

These denticles stop tiny ocean creatures from sticking to sharks' skin. Sharks can glide faster through the water if they are clean.
DENTICLES: PASCAL DEYNAT/ODONTOBASE/WIKIMEDIA. ORG/CC BY-SA 3.0
SHARK: WILDESTANIMAL/SHUTTERSTOCK.COM

LIGHT IT UP, FIREFLY

The flickering light of fireflies at night seems positively magical. The science behind the glow is pure chemistry—at least, that's what researchers used to think. But it turns out the shape of the firefly's body is also important. Examining fireflies under a special high-powered microscope revealed a pattern of jagged scales that stops light from being reflected back inward, allowing more light to escape and making fireflies brighter.

Copying the fireflies, scientists designed a special scale-shaped coating for **LED** lights that increased their brightness by

Imagine if you could light your home with a lamp filled with glowing bacteria, like these Photobacterium phosphoreum.
KPWANGKANONT/SHUTTERSTOCK.COM

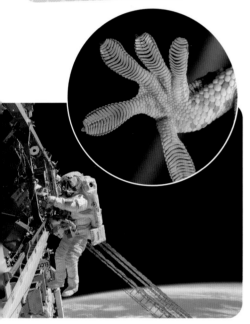

Geckos reach for the stars! NASA is creating robots that can "catch" space junk, such as old satellites, using an adhesive inspired by geckos.

GECKO: MR.B-KING/SHUTTERSTOCK.COM
SATELLITE: COURTESY OF NASA

In some places, getting clean water is harder than just turning on the tap. These kids are fetching water in Turbat, Kazakhstan.
DINOZZAVER/DREAMSTIME.COM

more than half but used the same amount of energy. There are more than 2,000 species of fireflies around the world—there may be even better scale shapes waiting to be found.

SUPER-STICKY GECKO TAPE

Have you ever dreamed of climbing straight up a wall like a gecko can? Geckos are likable lizards with a sticky trick—hairy toes. Gecko toes have big pads covered by millions of tiny hairs, each of which splits off into even tinier bristles. These tiny hairs can get so close to walls and ceilings that the molecules of the hair and the surface are drawn to each other, creating suction and making the gecko's toes stick to whatever it wants to climb. Geckos can turn the stickiness of their feet on and off as often as they like—no glue needed.

By copying gecko feet, scientists have made tape that lets a person climb glass. A piece of gecko tape the size of an index card can hold up a grizzly bear or a Spanish fighting bull. It detaches easily, can be used lots of times and doesn't leave any gooey glue residue behind.

CATCH THE RAIN(WATER)

Fog beetles live in the dry, sandy desert of Namibia. Like all animals, they need water to live. The fog on cold mornings provides the only water. The beetles climb steep sand dunes and turn their rear ends to the wind to get a drink. They trap water in tiny grooves and bumps on their shells, which have channels that carry the water to the beetle's mouth.

Like the beetles, we all need fresh, clean water to survive, but people in desert communities often don't have enough. People are copying beetles to capture water in new ways. In the deserts of Namibia, Chile and Israel, people are now harvesting water from fog using huge nets that collect water droplets.

STRONGER THAN STEEL, MADE LIKE YOGURT

Spider silk is so thin it's almost invisible, but it's stronger than steel. When huge insects hit a spiderweb, it stretches and snaps back, but it doesn't break. A human-scale web could stop an airplane.

Spiders spin this amazing material inside their own bodies, using water instead of the toxic chemicals we use to make fabric.

Scientists are mimicking spider silk, using microbes to produce the same basic material. The silk is strong and stretchy, and making it doesn't require a lot of energy or chemicals, similar to adding microbes to milk to make yogurt. Best of all, because it's made of protein instead of petroleum, it is **compostable** and won't end up in a landfill. Imagine composting your running shoes when you grow out of them. You'd just put them in the sink and add a packet of enzyme powder!

Using the superpower of spider silk, designers are making compostable winter jackets, yarn, surgical sutures, bulletproof vests and even violin strings! One day spider silk might even be part of buildings and cars.

Would violin strings made of spider silk sound different?
SPIDER: DAVE CLENDENAN
VIOLINIST: DENISPRODUCTION.COM/SHUTTERSTOCK.COM

ROACHES TO THE RESCUE!

Cockroaches. They're kind of, well, creepy. They sneak into buildings through the tiniest cracks. You can stomp on them, but they always seem to escape. They can also withstand pressure equal to 900 times their body weight without being hurt.

If you're a firefighter responding to an emergency such as a collapsed building, you need to find survivors fast. They might be injured or running out of air to breathe. Imagine if you could send in super-speedy, flexible, almost-impossible-to-crush search-and-rescue robots whose design was inspired by cockroaches. They could run straight up walls. Navigate rubble. Even if they lost a foot, they wouldn't slow down.

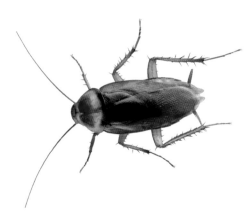

Even when squished down to half their height, cockroaches don't slow down. Instead they run with their legs straight out to the side.
GRAFISSIMO/GETTY IMAGES

Imagine sending in a swarm of cockroach-inspired robots to help rescuers find safe entry points and locate survivors.

Scientists at the University of Berkeley mimicked the robust cockroach to design a robot that might one day help rescue people trapped after earthquakes and other natural disasters. The robot cockroach can easily squeeze through cracks because it's only half an inch tall and can be squashed to the height of just two stacked nickels. Fitted with cameras or other sensors, such robots might one day be able to help lead firefighters to survivors.

Many animals have inspired new designs. There are robotic arms patterned after elephant trunks, which have 40,000 muscles. Incredibly precise and flexible, these robots can be used in factories, laboratories and even hospitals.

CAT-BRAINED COMPUTING

Cats seem to know when it's time for you to come home, and they're often waiting by the front door. How they figure that out is a mystery. All brains—cat, human, elephant, you name it—contain billions of nerve cells, called **neurons**, that can connect to many other neurons. These complicated networks of connections make brains faster than our fastest computers, and they can work on more problems at the same time. A computer engineer named Wei Lu wants to build a computer the way nature builds a brain. He chose a cat brain because it is simpler than a human brain but still has more connections than our fastest computer.

By mimicking the networks in a cat brain, he hopes to build a computer that can make thousands of connections in less time. His goal is that one day the computer might be the size of a two-liter pop bottle instead of filling a room. Today's super-computers, the most powerful type of computer, are incredibly fast, yet they're still 83 times slower than a cat's brain. But if you want help from a cat's brain anytime soon, you'll need to ask a cat.

"Your move!"
DAVE CLENDENAN

BATTERIES FROM BEACHES?

Batteries power our world, from cell phones and remote-control toys to laptops and electric cars. All batteries, even rechargeable ones, eventually have to be disposed of. One of the big problems with batteries is that they're full of toxic and rare materials, such as cobalt.

Blooms of green algae clog beaches around the world, and there's definitely no shortage of this gunky substance. But what if algae could be the answer for a new, metal-free battery? Researchers at Uppsala University in Sweden are making a battery with no heavy metals or toxic chemicals by harvesting the algae and coating it with a thin layer that conducts electricity.

Scientists hope that one day algae batteries might be used just like regular batteries. Another bonus is that algae batteries can be charged in just 11 seconds. Maybe one day algae batteries will power a battery revolution!

NATURE'S JOURNAL

Kim once had a roommate, Becky, who loved to garden. One day when Kim was spreading compost on the tomato bed, she found a metal zipper. When Kim asked her what it was doing in the compost, Becky replied, "Oh, that must be from my jeans. I compost them when they get too many holes." Sure enough, the next week Kim saw Becky putting her old jeans in the compost bin. Because jeans are made of cotton, they break down quickly, leaving only zippers, buttons and little pocket-corner rivets behind.

Kim's old jeans will be a tasty snack for her garden.
DOUGLAS WOOLCOCK

CHAPTER FOUR

Reducing Our Footprint

What does the city of the future look like in your imagination? IURII/SHUTTERSTOCK.COM

We can change how we design things to create a better world. When we build our cities, we need to learn to look around us to see how we can fit ourselves into nature instead of changing it to suit ourselves. Designers, engineers and kids are already learning from nature and building a better future.

LOOKING BACK TO LOOK FORWARD

The science of biomimicry is new, but the idea of it is not. Indigenous Peoples around the globe have been taking clues from nature and designing their lifestyles to fit into natural patterns for thousands of years. Architects, designers and scientists are beginning to tap into this wisdom.

Julia Watson, an architect and designer, traveled the world to learn natural design from Indigenous communities and found many ideas for building more sustainable towns and cities. In northeastern India, in the state of Meghalaya, it is so rainy that wooden and steel bridges rot or rust very quickly. So the people there grow living bridges instead. They plant rubber trees on either side of a river or canyon. Rubber trees grow above-ground

FACT:
In 2018, Costa Rica, a Central American country, ran for 300 days on 100 percent renewable energy!

Some of these rubber-tree bridges are hundreds of years old. DHRITIPURNA/SHUTTERSTOCK.COM

roots that support the main trunk. By wrapping these long, flexible roots around another piece of wood or bamboo, Khasi and Jaintia builders are able to guide them across to the other side, weaving them together, and then plant them again. The roots intertwine and even fuse together. Instead of rotting, these bridges thrive on the rain and grow stronger over time.

Trees have offered building solutions to people all over the globe. The birch tree, common in eastern North America, has a smooth white bark that can be peeled away in paper-thin layers that are surprisingly tough and waterproof. The Algonquin Peoples of the region that today encompasses southern Ontario and Quebec and parts of the northeastern United States traditionally used birch bark in many ways, including to make canoes, food-storage containers, rope and covering for their homes, called wigwams. Sheets of birch bark were placed over a wooden frame, then held in place with rope. Tree bark reflects just the right amount of sunlight while absorbing the optimal amount of heat. This characteristic makes for built-in temperature control.

FACT:
Scientists have found fungi that can digest plastic. Maybe one day fungi will be able to help us get rid of our plastic garbage!

Birch bark provided families with a local source of waterproof material to keep their homes warm and dry. Today people are investigating how the use of tree bark for roof shingles and siding could help homes use less energy.

NATURE'S BUILDING BLOCKS

We use *concrete* to build skyscrapers, highways and bridges, but the making of concrete releases tons of carbon dioxide emissions. It would be good for our planet if one day we could produce a building material that is less polluting than concrete.

You might not think of a chicken as a master builder, but it can build an eggshell in 18 hours. It's built at body temperature, creates no waste and is tougher than human-made ceramic. Building bridges or buildings with eggshells might sound a little far-fetched. But eggshells, and other *biominerals* such as bones and seashells, are basically natural concrete.

Scientists are experimenting with eggshells in the laboratory to see what could be used as a building material. While the science is still new, it's exciting to dream big about the future.

In the meantime, we can use biomimicry to fix the concrete already out there. When concrete cracks, it's difficult to repair. Microbiologist Hendrik Jonkers wondered if he could make concrete last longer. He found a solution. A type of limestone-producing bacteria called *Bacillus pseudofirmus* is mixed into the concrete. The bacteria can stay inactive for up to 200 years. When water seeps into cracks in the concrete, it wakes up the limestone-producing bacteria, which fill the cracks.

The bacteria can mend cracks up to 0.04 inches (1 millimeter) wide, and in Ecuador, a rainy tropical country, engineers have built a canal and irrigation system using self-healing concrete. The bacteria have been healing cracked concrete in other countries too.

Scientists have discovered that eggshells have built-in sun protection. People are experimenting with adding eggshells to building materials to help them better withstand the sun's rays.
MOONBORNE/SHUTTERSTOCK.COM

FACT:
We're running out of sand. We use 50 billion tons (45 billion metric tons) per year of marine sand—sand from river bottoms and beaches—to make concrete, glass and computer chips. Desert sand won't cut it, because the grains are too round.

FOREST IN THE CITY

It would be pretty neat if our cities, instead of having so much concrete everywhere, could be designed more like forests. In the rainy city of Seattle, the nonprofit group Urban Greenprint has teamed up with engineers, biologists and city planners to figure out how to reduce flooding and keep pollutants from being washed into the nearby ocean.

They studied the ecosystem to find out how the forest is able to hold on to so much rain. They observed that the many layers of tree leaves slow the rain, and the moss and tree bark hold water like a sponge. They also noticed that pine needles spear raindrops, breaking them into smaller droplets to create forest mist instead of drops falling to the ground and washing away soil.

With these observations in mind, they found solutions for the city environment. To slow the rain, designers can mimic the forest's layers by building canopies and screens on buildings. Wire sculptures can mimic the ability of pine needles to split raindrops and increase evaporation. Sculptures can not only help the city function more like a forest, but are also neat to look at. By learning how forest ecosystems thrive, we can build cities that fit into nature better and can survive extreme weather.

What if we cleaned our water with actual live plants instead of water-treatment plants? Cleaning up the wastewater from our buildings and factories is often expensive and time-consuming. Even a miniature wetland, a raft full of plants set adrift in dirty water, can act as a natural water purifier. Bacteria team with plant roots to eat nasty chemicals in the water and pull out heavy metals, such as copper and lead, or even oil and grease.

These supertrees collect rainwater, generate solar power and provide beautiful green space for the residents of Singapore.
S-F/SHUTTERSTOCK.COM

Plants grown on buildings are called living walls. Not only are they beautiful, but they can help to slow rainwater and improve air quality by absorbing pollutants.
ALISON HANCOCK/SHUTTERSTOCK.COM

Jorge Zapote, Mitchell Weber, Xi Cheng and Michelle Zhou worked together to create the WindChill
RILEY BRANDT/UNIVERSITY OF CALGARY

In Harare, the capital of Zimbabwe, the Eastgate Shopping Centre was modeled after self-cooling termite mounds like these ones. It has no air-conditioning or heating, but stays comfortable year-round.
KAREL STIPEK/SHUTTERSTOCK.COM

CHILL OUT...

If you leave it on the counter, milk turns sour. And if the power goes out, your parents probably worry about what will happen to all that food in the fridge. But there are places where most people can't afford to have a fridge in their house.

A group of University of Calgary students copied the way animals keep cool in nature to construct a fridge that doesn't need to be plugged in. They looked at kangaroos, elephants, bees and even termites for inspiration. Their design, the WindChill, is cheap, portable and needs only a tiny trickle of electricity from a solar panel.

Inspired by termite mounds, whose shape directs cooling breezes inside, the team used a funnel to channel fresh air into the fridge naturally, without using energy. Next, mimicking how kangaroos lick their forearms and let the spit evaporate and how elephants spray themselves with water and use their ears to gently fan their bodies, the air is directed through a spiral of copper pipe that is misted with water and cooled by a solar-powered fan. When the water evaporates, it cools the air in the pipes—just like you're cooled by running through a sprinkler on a breezy day. The cool air flows into a food-storage chamber placed underground, an idea inspired by how meerkats burrow into the ground to escape the heat. What a cool idea!

Elephants' ability to sense vibrations with their feet and trunks has inspired research into new devices to help people hear better.
PAULA FRENCH/SHUTTERSTOCK.COM

GERMS DYED MY CLOTHES

Colorful clothes are beautiful, but fabric dyeing is one of the most polluting industries. The runoff from clothing factories sometimes dyes whole rivers! Designers are experimenting with biomimicry-based ways of making funky clothes. Some are using germs or bacteria. Bacteria produce pigments from pink to yellow to blue. So, some designers asked, what would happen if we grew these colorful bacteria on fabric?

It turns out they dye the clothes! Clothing designer Natsai Audrey Chieza is dyeing silk scarves by putting them in petri dishes with *Streptomyces coelicolor,* a bacteria found on plant roots. The bacteria will dye the fabric blue or pink or a shade

NATURE'S JOURNAL

Kim's friend Suzanne teaches biology at university. She also likes to dye fabric and make art. She asked her students to test dyeing using microbes, and this is what they did!

Can you imagine stuffing your shirt into a petri dish and using bacteria to dye it?
SUZANNE JONESON

somewhere in between, depending on how much acid is in the mix. The process uses hardly any water, needs no heavy metals to fix the dyes in the clothes and doesn't pollute the rivers.

One of the interesting problems to solve with this method is how to work with the bacteria. How do you tell bacteria what pattern to make? They don't have ears! But the current process means every scarf is unique.

FISHY WIND FARMS

When scientists are trying to solve problems using biomimicry, they look for animals with unusual abilities. For example, schools of fish dart through the ocean without ever bumping into each other. An engineer named John Dabiri observed that fish swimming in schools boost each other with tiny whirlpools of energy called vortexes. He wondered how they move so well together and whether he could learn from them how to build better wind turbines.

Wind farms take up a lot of land, because if you place traditional propeller-style wind turbines too close together, they don't generate as much power. This makes it hard to find enough space to build new wind farms.

Using his observations of how schools of fish swim, Dabiri designed a new style of wind turbine. Instead of propellers it uses a vertical rotor. These turbines are smaller and can be placed closer to each other. The blades spin like a coin on its side, and, like a school of fish, each rotor gains energy from its neighbor, boosting wind production by more than 10 times that of the traditional design.

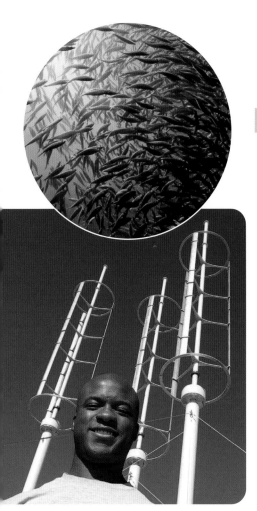

John Dabiri has made his invention come to life, from his first spark of inspiration—watching how fish swim—through to the installation of efficient wind turbines!

WATCH, LEARN, INVENT

Kids around the world are observing nature and finding new ways to reduce our footprint.

Lion under the sun

Richard Turere, a Maasai herder from Kenya, was responsible for his family's cows at age nine. His family lived at the southern end of Nairobi National Park, where there are no fences. Wildlife, including lions, could roam freely into his community, causing conflict between lions and humans—several lions had been killed. Richard's biggest challenge was that lions came every night and attacked the cattle, his family's main source of income. They were losing many cows each week, which they couldn't afford. Richard tried lighting fires to scare the lions away. He set up a scarecrow. Neither worked. Then he noticed that when he walked around the cowshed with a flashlight, the lions didn't attack. Knowing that lions are afraid of people, he concluded that they associated moving lights with humans. Richard tinkered with a few basic electronic parts he had. He built a series of flashing lights, powered by a solar panel, and set them around the enclosure. The lions stayed away, and Richard was able to go to bed instead of patrolling the pen all night.

Now households across Kenya use Richard's "lion lights" to protect their cattle and sheep. Richard's creative lighting system that mimics a human with a flashlight helps both humans and lions.

Richard's Lion Lights have been installed in more than 750 homesteads in Kenya.
RIXIPIX/GETTY IMAGES

Saharan silver ants are also the world's fastest ants. They can sprint a distance 108 times their own body length in just one second.
BJØRN CHRISTIAN TØRRISSEN/WIKIMEDIA.ORG
/CC BY-SA 3.0

One tough ant

The Saharan silver ant lives in the Sahara Desert in Africa, where burning temperatures as hot as 122°F (50°C) make life difficult. But this ant has a few tricks up its sleeve. Under the midday sun, when all its predators are forced to stay in the shade or risk death, the Saharan silver ant leaves its burrow in search of food. It can do this because it has a built-in heat shield—the ultimate sunshade. The ant is covered in special hairs that reflect the sun and disperse body heat, keeping it cool (or, at least, cool enough not to melt under the hot sun).

White roofs, like these on houses in Florida, reflect heat, keeping the homes cooler.
SPWIDOFF/SHUTTERSTOCK.COM

More than one billion people around the world live in deserts. Keeping cool is a serious challenge, as heat waves are life-threatening to many people. Millions of people who live in the deserts of northwest India and North Africa don't have access to air-conditioning.

To help desert dwellers stay cool, a group of middle-schoolers from Hawaii invented the SunTile, a roofing tile for desert homes inspired by the Saharan silver ant, as well as the desert scorpion and a bee's hexagon-shaped honeycomb. The team placed first in the middle-school category in the Biomimicry Institute's Youth Design Challenge in 2018.

The SunTile is a hexagonal tile with prisms that mimic the hairs of the Saharan silver ant, reflecting sunlight to keep the roof cooler. Tiny grooves inspired by the desert scorpion's ability to repel sand help protect the tile from erosion, and the hexagonal shape helps spread the weight evenly, like a bee's honeycomb.

Going bananas

Plastics are useful for many things. The main problem is that most of them aren't compostable. Making a new, natural, compostable plastic was the task that Elif Bilgin, from Istanbul, Turkey, set for herself at age 16. She had heard about making plastic out of potatoes. Because people can eat potatoes, she decided to use something that was going to be thrown away anyway—banana peels.

She tested methods for two years, dipping the peels in disinfectant, boiling and puréeing them, then putting them in petri dishes to bake. She performed a dozen trials before she got a plastic that held together and didn't decay, doing it all in her kitchen. The plastic is simple enough to make at home. It could potentially be used to insulate copper wires or to cover a prosthetic limb. As a bonus, Elif also became a pro at making banana cupcakes and banana splits!

THE LAND OF TOMORROW

It might seem impossible to build with eggshells, power everything with sunlight and use no plastic. Once upon a time, making materials that would carry humans into space or devices that would instantly connect people around the globe seemed impossible. But humans made these things happen. We can do the impossible again! Only this time our challenge is to use biomimicry to fit ourselves back into the natural cycle. When you put this book down, we hope you will walk outside, look at nature with new eyes and think about how you could help everyone learn from nature.

What will you invent to change the world? MONKEY BUSINESS IMAGES/SHUTTERSTOCK.COM

Acknowledgments

An amazing number of people helped to make this book possible! Thanks to the incredible team at Orca for such a remarkable commitment to producing quality books, in particular our editor, Kirstie Hudson. The seed for this book was planted when Kim read Janine Benyus's book *Biomimicry* more than 20 years ago and never stopped thinking about it.

Kim and Megan have been writer buddies for more than 10 years, and this sure was a fun project to work on together. Thanks to our wonderful readers who offered their time, wisdom and eagle eyes, including Nina Giuliani, Amy Tsang, Todd Rowlatt, Sean Woolcock and Suzanne Joneson.

Writing this book gifted us with the opportunity to learn so much about hopeful, exciting innovations that are changing our world for the better. While there isn't space here to name them all, we'd like to acknowledge all the bright thinkers, inventors and dreamers working in the field of biomimicry, especially those who shared the photos and information that helped make this book possible.

Thanks to Kim's family for the thousands (and thousands) of times they took her to the library when she was a kid. And, most of all, thanks to Douglas, Theo, Dave and Owen for not minding all the times we snuck off to write down just one more idea.

All these new inventions and innovations are a great reason to celebrate! PALIDACHAN/SHUTTERSTOCK.COM

Resources

Print

Becker, Helaine. *Zoobots: Wild Robots Inspired by Real Animals.* Toronto: Kids Can Press, 2014.

Campbell, Sarah C. *Growing Patterns: Fibonacci Numbers in Nature.* Honesdale, PA: Boyds Mills Press, an imprint of Highlights, 2010.

Campbell, Sarah C. *Mysterious Patterns: Finding Fractals in Nature.* Honesdale, PA: Boyds Mills Press, an imprint of Highlights, 2014.

Kaner, Etta. *Wild Buildings and Bridges: Architecture Inspired by Nature.* Toronto: Kids Can Press, 2018.

Lee, Dora. *Biomimicry: Inventions Inspired by Nature.* Toronto: Kids Can Press, 2011.

Watson, Galadriel. *Running Wild: Awesome Animals in Motion.* Toronto: Annick Press, 2020.

Online

30 Animals That Made Us Smarter: BBC World Service: podnews.net/podcast/1455717403

Biomimicry Institute: biomimicry.org

How We Make Stuff: made2bmadeagain.org

The Kid Should See This: thekidshouldseethis.com

The Story of Stuff: storyofstuff.org

Think Like a Tree: wired.com/video/series/think-like-a-tree

Youth Biomimicry Design Challenge: youthchallenge.biomimicry.org

TED Talks

Barnett, Heather. "What humans can learn from semi-intelligent slime." June 2014. 12:00.
ted.com/talks/heather_barnett_what_humans_can_learn_from_semi_intelligent_slime

Benyus, Janine. "Biomimicry in action." July 2009. 17:24.
ted.com/talks/janine_benyus_biomimicry_in_action?language=en

Benyus, Janine. "Biomimicry's surprising lessons from nature's engineers." February 2005. 23:00.
ted.com/talks/janine_benyus_biomimicry_s_surprising_lessons_from_nature_s_engineers

Full, Robert. "The secrets of nature's grossest creatures, channeled into robots." March 2014. 4:57.
ted.com/talks/robert_full_the_secrets_of_nature_s_grossest_creatures_channeled_into_robots

Pawlyn, Michael. "Using nature's genius in architecture." November 2010. 13:31.
ted.com/talks/michael_pawlyn_using_nature_s_genius_in_architecture

Glossary

aerodynamic—a shape or design that allows an object to move smoothly and quickly through air

algae—plantlike organisms, found chiefly in water, that have no roots, stems or leaves and make their own food through photosynthesis

antibiotics—medicines produced by bacteria or fungi, used to stop or slow the growth of harmful germs in humans and animals

bacteria—tiny, single-celled organisms found everywhere around us that can be harmful or beneficial

biomimicry—the process of designing and producing materials, structures and systems that are modeled on living organisms and natural processes while taking care of our home, Planet Earth

biominerals—substances that combine minerals (like iron or calcium) with biological materials (like proteins); bones, teeth, shells and corals are all biominerals

carbon—a nonmetallic chemical element found in all plants and animals and which is also part of substances such as coal and oil

carbon dioxide—a colorless, odorless gas breathed out by animals and absorbed from the air by plants; it is also formed by burning fossil fuels and is a greenhouse gas

cell—the smallest unit with the basic properties of life; every living thing is made up of cells, from one-celled bacteria to animals with billions of cells

chitin—a tough material that forms the hard parts of many animals, including insect exoskeletons, fungal cell walls, octopus beaks and fish scales

climate change—a long-term shift in global and regional weather and climate patterns caused by increased levels of carbon dioxide in the air due to the burning of fossil fuels

compostable—capable of disintegrating into natural elements that leave no trace in the soil

concrete—a building material made from a mix of rocks, sand, cement and water that can be poured into forms and sets hard as stone

conduct—convey or transmit the flow of an electric current

enzyme—a protein molecule in plants and animals that speeds biochemical reactions and can build up or break down other molecules

exoskeleton—a hard outer covering that supports and protects the bodies of some animals that do not have internal skeletons, such as insects and spiders

fossil fuels—materials formed from the fossilized remains of plants and animals, converted to oil, coal or natural gas by heat and pressure in the earth's crust over hundreds of millions of years

fungi—(plural of *fungus*) living organisms that are neither plant nor animal, such as yeasts, molds and mushrooms

germs—tiny organisms, which scientists call microbes, that cause disease in a plant or animal

heavy metals—metallic chemical elements that have a high density and are toxic or poisonous at low concentrations, such as mercury, lead and arsenic

LED—light-emitting diode, an energy-efficient type of light

linen—a strong, absorbent and quick-drying natural fabric that is made from the long, tough fibers in flax plants

malaria—a serious disease caused by a tiny organism and spread through mosquito bites; common in many tropical regions, it causes fever and sometimes death

microbes—organisms so small they are visible only under a microscope, such as bacteria, fungi, algae, protozoa and viruses

minerals—naturally occurring substances that do not come from an animal or a plant and are found on Earth's surface in rocks, sands and soils, as well as underground

molecule—two or more atoms joined together; a molecule is the smallest possible unit of a substance.

neurons—specialized cells that transmit nerve impulses by electricity

nitrogen—a colorless, tasteless gas that makes up most of Earth's atmosphere

particulate matter—tiny particles of solid or liquid matter that when released into the atmosphere can make the air we breathe dirty; they are linked to diseases like lung cancer

photosynthesis—the process by which green plants absorb energy from sunlight and turn water and carbon dioxide into sugar for food

phytomining—the process of producing a metal "crop" by growing and subsequently harvesting plants that absorb specific metals from soil into their tissues

pigment—a compound that gives a particular color to an organism or substance

protein—a long chain of amino acids that is an essential part of all living organisms, especially in such parts as muscle and hair

self-assembling materials—materials with the ability to spontaneously put together organized patterns and structures

silk—natural fabric made from the fiber that silkworms spin to form cocoons

solar panel—a device that absorbs the sun's rays and converts them into electricity

synthetic fiber—a human-made textile fiber made from chemicals and produced in a laboratory, not harvested from nature; for example, nylon is produced from petroleum, a fossil fuel

toxic—dangerous or poisonous to humans or animals

vaccines—preparations of microorganisms, either dead or weakened, that are given to people to help their bodies fight off specific diseases

vortexes—whirling masses of fluid, air or energy, such as whirlpools, whirlwinds, cyclones or tornados; vortexes create a vacuum in the center that draws things inward

Index

Page numbers in **bold** *indicate an image caption.*

abalone shells, 18
activism: less waste, 15, 31, 41; resources, 23, 43
aerodynamic, 25, 44
algae, 19, 31, 44
antibiotics, 27, 44
ants and termites, **18**, 36, 39–40
architecture: bridges, 32–33; and concrete, 34, 44; urban, **32**, 35, **36**
armor, cloth, 10

bacteria: bioluminescence, 6, **27**; defined, 44; for dyeing fabric, 37–38; limestone-producing, 34; use of, **22**, 23
bananas, 14, 40
batteries, metal-free, 31
Bilgin, Elif, 40
bioluminescence, 19, **27**, 28
biomimicry: defined, 8, 44; in design, 6, 34–38; examples of, 24–31; green chemistry, 19; in materials, 10–13, 17–19; and problem solving, 8–9, 24, 41
biominerals, 34, 44
birch bark, 33–34
birds, **15**, 25, 34
brain structure, 20, 30
branching patterns, 21; roads, 22
bridges: by ants, **18**; of trees, 32–33
broccoli pattern, **20**
building solutions: and concrete, 34; heat shields, 40; trees, 32–34; urban design, 35
butterfly, wing design, 16

carbon, 18, 44
carbon dioxide, 17, 34, 44
casein plastic, 12
cats, brain structure, 30
cell phones, 15
cells, 20, 30, 44
ceramics, 18
chameleons, **21**
Cheng, Xi, **36**
Chieza, Natsai Audrey, 37

children: invention and design, 9, 39–41; lunch of a pioneer, 14
chitin, 17, 44
cities: design, 32, 35; water supply, 15, 35
climate change, 17, 44
clothing: compostable, 31; dyes, 10–11, 37–38; fasteners, 19; natural materials, 10–12; and spider silk, 29; synthetic fibers, 12–13; that repels stains, 24
cochineal insects, **11**
cockroach design, 29–30
colors: pigments, 16, 37, 45; purple dye, 10–11
compostable: defined, 44; materials, 29, 31; natural cycles, 16–17; plastic problem, 13
composting bins, **18**, 31
computers, 15, 30, 40
concrete, 34, 44
Costa Rica, 32
cotton, 10, 31

Dabiri, John, 38
de Mestral, George, 19
desert conditions: heat shields, 39–40; self-cooling units, 36–37; and water supply, 15, 28
diatoms, 20
dyes, 10–11, 37–38

eggshell material, 34
electric equipment: appliances, 13; batteries, 31; computers, 15, 30, 40; e-waste, 15; hearing aids, **37**; lighting, 27–28, 39; self-cooling units, 36–37
elephants, 30, 37
enzymes, 19, 29, 44
exoskeletons, 17, 44

fabric: armor, 10; compostable, 31; dyes, 10–11, 37–38; fasteners, 19; natural materials, 10–12; and spider silk, 29; synthetic fibers, 12–13; that

repels stains, 24
fern fronds, 21
Fibonacci sequence, 21
filtration systems, 22–23, 35
fireflies, 19, 27–28
fleece fabric, 13
fog beetles, 28
food production: gardening, 14, **17**; imported food, 14–15; lunch of a pioneer, 14; protecting livestock, 39
fossil fuels, 8, 17, 44
fractal patterns, 20
fungi (fungus), 16, 33, 44

Ganges River delta, **21**
garbage, 6, 8, 13, 33
gardening, 14, **17**
gecko, feet design, 28
germs, 6, 23, 37, 44–45
glue, 9, 10, 19
Gray, Adeline, 12
green chemistry, 19

hair combs, **17**
Hawaii, beaches, 13
hawksbill sea turtles, **17**
hearing, 21, **37**
heat: self-cooling units, 36–37; shields, 39–40
heavy metals, 23, 31, 35, 38, 45
hippopotamuses, 24

India, tree bridges, 32–33
Indigenous Peoples, 32–34
insects: adaptations, 16, 26, 28, 39–40; bioluminescence, 19, 27–28; as builders, **18**, 36; dyes from, **11**; spider silk, 29; structure of, 17, 29–30

Jonkers, Hendrik, 34

kangaroos, 36–37
Kevlar, 12
kingfishers, 25

Index (continued)

Las Vegas, water supply, 15
LED lights, 27–28, 45
linen, 10, 45
lion lights, 39
lotus plants, 24
Lu, Wei, 30

malaria, 11, 45
marine life: diatoms, 20; and glue, 19; schools of fish, 38; sea turtles, **17**; shark skin design, 27; shell design, 6, 18, 21
medicine: germ-repelling surfaces, 27; needles, 26; preservation of vaccines, 26–27
metals: heavy, 23, 31, 35, 38, 45; in trash, **15**
microbes, 23, 29, 37, 45
microplastics, **13**
minerals, 18, 45; biominerals, 34, 44
molds, slime, 22
molecules, 18, 20, 28, 45
mosquitos, 26
mother-of-pearl, **18**
mustard plants, 20

nature: cycles of, 8, 16–20; design of, 7, **22**, 23, **24**, 31; patterns of, 20–21
nautilus shell, **21**
needles, medical, 26
neurons, 30, 45
nitrogen, 18, 45
nylon, 12

Okefenokee Swamp, 23
oxygen supply, 18, **20**

painted lady butterfly, **16**
particulate matter, 23, 45
Perkin, William Henry, 11
Peru, natural dyes, **11**
photosynthesis, 8, 16–17, 45
phytomining, 23, 45
pigments, 16, 37, 45

plants: building solutions, 32–34, 35; cleaning water and soil, 23, 35; defenses, 20; design, 8–9, 21; and fabric design, 24; living walls, **35**; natural fibers, 10; photosynthesis, 8, 16–17, 45; and solar panel design, 8
plastic: compostable, 40; and fleece fabric, 13; and fungi, 33; microplastics, **13**; from milk proteins, 12; use of, 13
pollution: air, 23; and concrete, 34; metals and chemicals, 31; toxic materials, 8, 14–15, 31, 35, 45; water, 35, 37–38
polyester, 12–13
protein, 18, 45
purple dye, 10–11

refrigeration: alternatives, 26–27, 36–37; impact of, 14–15
renewable energy: impact of, 32; solar, 9, 18, 45; wind, 38
resources, 23, 43
robot design, **28**, 29–30
Romanesco broccoli, **20**
roof tiles, **40**
rubber tree, bridges, 32–33

Saharan silver ant, 39–40
sand, supply, 34
Seattle, urban design, 35
self-assembling materials, 18, 45
shark skin, design of, 27
shells, 6, 18, 21
shock absorbers, 26
silk, 12, 45
Singapore, urban design, **35**
slime molds, 22
snails: and dyes, 11; shells, 18
soil, filtration, 22–23
solar power: cells, 18; panels, 9, 45
spider silk, 29
spiral patterns, 21
stormwater management, 35

SunTile roofing, 40
synthetic fibers, 12–13, 45

tardigrades (water bears), 26–27
technologies: and biomimicry, 41; green chemistry, 19; impact of, 9
termite mounds, 36
toothbrush materials, 10
toxic materials, 8, 14–15, 31, 35, 45
train design, 25
transportation: of food, 14–15; train design, 25; of vaccines, 26–27
tree bark, 33–34
tree frogs, 7
trehalose sugar, 26–27
Turere, Richard, 39

urban design, 15, 32, 35, **36**

vaccines, 26–27, 45
velcro fasteners, 19
vortexes, 21, 38, 45

water: distribution, 15, 21, **28**; filtration, 22–23; harvesting, 28, **35**; and urban design, 35
Watson, Julia, 32–33
Weber, Mitchell, **36**
wetlands, 23, 35
WindChill, self-cooling units, 36–37
wind turbine, design, 38
wire sculptures, 35
woodpeckers, 26

Zapote, Jorge, **36**
Zhou, Michelle, **36**
Zimbabwe, urban design, **36**

MEGAN CLENDENAN is a freelance writer and editor. She is the author of *Offbeat*, a novel for young readers in the Orca Limelights series. Megan lives in North Vancouver, British Columbia, where she is surrounded by nature.

KIM RYALL WOOLCOCK has always loved books and biology. She has an honors degree in literature from UBC and a master's in biology from Duke University. A full-time science writer and editor, Kim lives on Salt Spring Island, British Columbia, with her family. This is her first book.